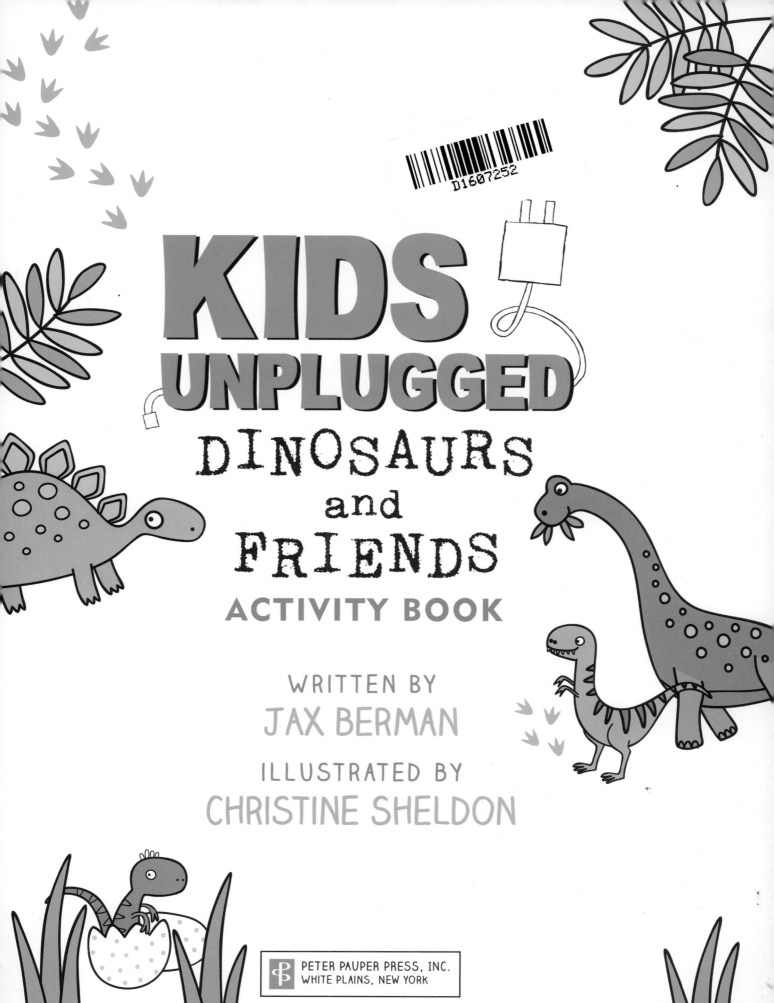

KIDS UNPLUGGED
DINOSAURS
and
FRIENDS
ACTIVITY BOOK

WRITTEN BY
JAX BERMAN

ILLUSTRATED BY
CHRISTINE SHELDON

PETER PAUPER PRESS, INC.
WHITE PLAINS, NEW YORK

PETER PAUPER PRESS
Fine Books and Gifts Since 1928

In 1928, at the age of twenty-two, Peter Beilenson
began printing books on a small press in the basement
of his parents' home in Larchmont, New York. Peter—
and later, his wife, Edna—sought to create fine books
that sold at "prices even a pauper could afford."

Today, still family owned and operated,
Peter Pauper Press continues to honor our
founders' legacy of quality, value, and fun for
big kids and small kids alike.

Illustrations © Christine Sheldon

Copyright © 2018 Peter Pauper Press, Inc.
Manufactured for Peter Pauper Press, Inc.
202 Mamaroneck Avenue
White Plains, NY 10601 USA

ISBN 978-1-4413-2599-0

Printed in China

Published in the United Kingdom and Europe by
Peter Pauper Press, Inc., c/o White Pebble International
Unit 2, Plot 11 Terminus Road
Chichester, West Sussex PO19 8TX, UK

7 6 5 4 3 2 1

Visit us at www.peterpauper.com

Attention Prehistoric Pals!

Ready to take a trip back in time? We're talking way before you, your parents, and even your teachers were born—all the way to the days of the dinosaurs! Millions of years before humans walked the earth, creatures known as the dinosaurs ruled the planet. Some walked on two legs, some on four, some were as small as the palm of your hand, and others were longer than a bus and taller than a giraffe! Most were feathered because—surprise!—all of them are related to modern-day birds!

In these pages, you'll learn all about these prehistoric critters, as well as a few other strange dinosaur-like creatures that shared their sky and ocean. Work your way through brain-teasing games, cool coloring pages, hands-on dino crafts, and other fun activities as you explore this ancient world.

SO TEST YOUR BRAIN POWER AND CREATIVITY AS YOU HEAD OUT ON AN APATOSAURUS-SIZED ADVENTURE— NO WIRES REQUIRED!

ANSWERS ARE IN THE BACK OF THIS BOOK.

MEET THE MESOZOIC

Dinosaurs as we know them lived a long, long time ago—from 231 million years ago to 66 million years ago, to be exact! This period was generally known as the **MESOZOIC ERA**, but scientists also divide it up into three parts: the **TRIASSIC PERIOD**, the **JURASSIC PERIOD**, and the **CRETACEOUS PERIOD**. (Dinosaurs came on the scene during the late Triassic specifically.) Each period is divided up based on really big events, such as continents shifting or mass extinctions.

TRIASSIC PERIOD

(237 MILLION YEARS AGO – 201 MILLION YEARS AGO)

Eoraptor

ADD EGGS TO THE NEST AND GIVE EORAPTOR SOME FRIENDS!

JURASSIC PERIOD

(200 MILLION YEARS AGO — 145 MILLION YEARS AGO)

DRAW IN SOME FERNS!

Stegosaurus

CRETACEOUS PERIOD

(145 MILLION YEARS AGO — 66 MILLION YEARS AGO)

Tyrannosaurus Rex
(T-rex)

DECORATE THESE DINOS!

THE WILD WORLD OF DINOSAURS

UNSCRAMBLE THE NAMES OF THE DINOSAURS ALL OVER THIS MAP TO DISCO[VER] WHO LIVED WHERE!

NORTH AMERICA

RCAOTIEPRTS

_ _ _ _ _ _ _ _ _ _ _

AFRI[CA]

SOUTH AMERICA

WORD BANK

Antarctopelta
Archaeopteryx
Brachiosaurus
Giganotosaurus
Minmi
Protoceratops
Triceratops
Velociraptor

NOOTIGAGSRSAUU

_ _ _ _ _ _ _ _ _ _ _ _ _

DID YOU KNOW? The world dinosaurs inhabited looked very different than ours. Way back in the Triassic period, all the continents were fused together into one giant landmass called Pangaea. Then, over millions of years, the continents drifted apart, first forming two large ones called Laurasia and Gondwana, until finally becoming the seven continents we know today.

XARPYTCAOHEER
_ _ _ _ _ _ _ _ _ _ _

LIVETROPCARO
_ _ _ _ _ _ _ _ _ _ _

ASIA

CTOSPEPRORAOT
_ _ _ _ _ _ _ _ _ _ _

ROPE

SCRABAIORSHUU
_ _ _ _ _ _ _ _ _ _ _ _

AUSTRALIA

NIIMM
_ _ _ _

ANTARCTICA

TARCLNATEOTAP
_ _ _ _ _ _ _ _ _ _ _

TRAVEL TO THE TRIASSIC!

Your mad scientist best friend has invented a time machine, and they've invited you to a prehistoric party! Look at the window to the Triassic period to figure out what the world you're about to visit is like. Then, pack a bag for a dino-mite weekend by picking what you need below.

☐ Sunscreen

☐ Sunglasses

☐ Snacks

☐ Boots
(heavy-duty, anti-dino-poop hiking boots!)

☐ Tennis racket

☐ Dino-repellent

☐ Toothbrush

☐ Flashlight

☐ Water bottle

☐ Bathing suit

☐ Basketball

☐ Kids Unplugged: Dinosaurs & Friends

☐ First-aid kit

☐ Fishing pole

☐ Raincoat

☐ Teddy bear

☐ A chicken

☐ Change of clothes

☐ Tent

Then color in this dino-filled landscape!

While dinosaurs appeared around 231 million years ago,
the Triassic period actually began around 252 million years ago.
Life in the sea flourished during the Triassic, but life on land
was hard. The climate was hot and dry, and not many plants besides
conifers (needle-leafed trees like pines) and ferns
grew there. However, dinosaurs shared the land with insects,
early mammals, and amphibians, including frogs.

ON THE HUNT

This Eoraptor is starving! Help it navigate through the Triassic deserts to a tasty snack!

DID YOU KNOW? Dinosaurs and other creatures can be classified into two groups based on what they eat. Meat-eaters are called carnivores, and plant-eaters are called herbivores. Most animals toda fall into these categories too, as well as a third category called omnivores (which means they eat both plants and animals).

A big clue is their teeth! Meat-eating dinosaurs had pointy, tearing teeth, and plant-eating dinosaurs had flat, grinding teeth. Dinosaurs that ate many different kinds of food tended to have a variety of tooth shapes!

Give this dino some teeth, then draw something for it to chow down on. Don't forget to color it in when you're done!

ATTACK OF THE BAGELSAURUS!

ASK AN ADULT TO HELP YOU WITH CUTTING!

YOU WILL NEED:

½ BAGEL
4 CARROT STICKS OR BABY CARROTS
½ BANANA
BAGEL TOPPINGS OF YOUR CHOICE
1 BLUEBERRY, GRAPE, OR OTHER
    SMALL FRUIT
SLICE OF CHEESE (OPTIONAL)

I. TOAST THE ½ BAGEL.
   (YOU CAN SHARE THE OTHER HALF WITH YOUR ADULT HELPER!)

2. WHEN IT'S COOL, SPREAD YOUR BAGEL TOPPINGS OVER YOUR BAGEL AND CUT IT IN HALF. ARRANGE HALF OF IT IN THE CENTER TO SERVE AS THE BODY. STICK THE OTHER HALF BEHIND IT (WHILE STAYING ON THE PLATE) TO SERVE AS THE TAIL.

3. ARRANGE THE CARROTS ALONG THE BOTTOM OF THE "BODY" BAGEL. THESE WILL BE ITS LEGS.

4. CUT THE TIP OFF THE BANANA AND PLACE THE LARGER PIECE WHERE YOU WANT THE DINOSAUR'S NECK TO GO. THEN, PLACE THE TIP AT THE OTHER END OF THE BANANA TO MAKE A HEAD.

5. ADD THE BLUEBERRY, GRAPE, OR OTHER SMALL FRUIT TO THE "HEAD" TO MAKE AN EYE.
   (TIP: YOU CAN "GLUE" THE EYE TO YOUR BANANA WITH HONEY.)

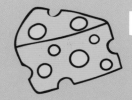

6. IF YOU'D LIKE, CUT THE SLICE OF CHEESE INTO SMALL PIECES, THEN ARRANGE THEM ALONG THE NECK AND BAGELS TO FORM A ROW OF FEROCIOUS SPIKES.

7. NOW **ROAR** LIKE A T-REX AND GOBBLE DOWN YOUR DINO!

DINO BY NUMBERS!

13

JURASSIC DOT-TO-DOT DINOSAURS

A LOT OF NEW PLANTS AND ANIMALS APPEARED DURING THE JURASSIC PERIOD. THIS INCLUDED EARLY BIRDS (AS WE KNOW THEM), MODERN LIZARDS, THERIANS (MAMMALS THAT COULD GIVE BIRTH TO LIVE YOUNG), AND NEW TYPES OF AMPHIBIANS, SUCH AS SALAMANDERS.

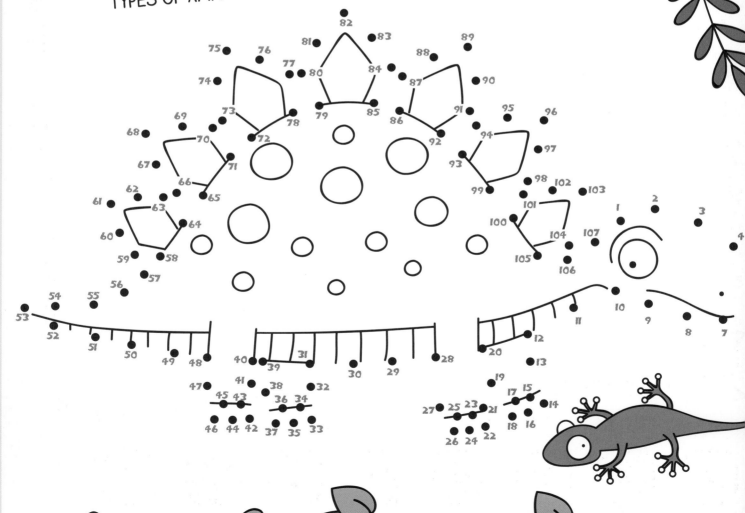

DID YOU KNOW?

THE FIRST DINOSAUR TO BE NAMED WAS MEGALOSAURUS, A GIANT CARNIVORE THAT LIVED IN WHAT'S NOW SOUTHERN ENGLAND. IT MAY EVEN HAVE BEEN THE FIRST ANCIENT DINOSAUR EVER DISCOVERED BY SCIENTISTS, AS A DRAWING OF ITS THIGH BONE APPEARED IN A BOOK IN 1676!

CONNECT THE DOTS TO REVEAL MEGALOSAURUS (ABOVE) AND STEGOSAURUS (LEFT). THEN COLOR THEM IN!

15

APATOSAURUS OF MY EYE

SPOT THE 10 DIFFERENCES BETWEEN THESE TWO PICTURES.
WHEN YOU FIND THEM, CIRCLE THEM, THEN COLOR THIS SCENE IN!

DEEP BLUE SAURS

Fill this page with other ancient aquatic friends (or food!) and then color them i

Ammonite

While dinosaurs dominated the land,
other creatures, such as plesiosaurs,
ichthyosaurs, and even turtles and sharks,
ruled the seas! On these pages, you'll
find an ammonite and
a plesiosaur.

Plesiosaur

KINGS OF THE SKY

Long ago, massive winged reptiles known as pterosaurs flew through the skies. Below, you'll find not only a few flying friends from the Jurassic period but also some familiar faces of today. Add decorations to these high flyers and color them in!

Archaeopteryx

DID YOU KNOW?
Archaeopteryx was a feathered dinosaur that lived in the late Jurassic period. It's also a "transitional fossil," or something that looked like both an ancient creature and its descendant. Archaeopteryx didn't just have the traits of an ancient dinosaur; it also had the traits of a modern bird!

The giant pterosaur Quetzalcoatlus was one of the largest flying creatures ever. Its wingspan could be up to 52 feet (15.9 m) wide. That's wider than a school bus is long!

Yi qi

Quetzalcoatlus

CRETACEOUS CREATURES!

Follow the steps below to draw the king of the Cretaceous period, Tyrannosaurus rex on the next page!

1 Start by drawing a wobbly oval shape.

2 Add on a tail and two lines for the neck.

3 Add on these simple shapes for the head and legs.

4 Erase the inside lines and add on two little arms and leg details.

5 Draw in the eye, teeth, and nostrils.

6 Finally, add some stripes and body detail to your T-rex!

Flowers first appeared on Earth during the Cretaceous period, the last third of the age of the dinosaurs, along with a variety of insects and new mammals. The world of the Cretaceous was a lot wetter, with inland seas that no longer exist. Some were home to all kinds of shellfish, including ammonites (ancestors to the octopus and squid).

WALK LIKE A DINOSAUR!

FOLLOW THE STEPS BELOW TO MAKE YOUR VERY OWN DINOSAUR SHOES SO YOU CAN WALK LIKE THE MIGHTY HADROSAUR!

YOU WILL NEED:

- 2 LONG TISSUE OR SHOE BOXES
- SCISSORS
- COLORFUL TISSUE OR CONSTRUCTION PAPER
- CONSTRUCTION PAPER (WHITE)
- GLUE
- TAPE
- ADULT HELPER (OPTIONAL)

1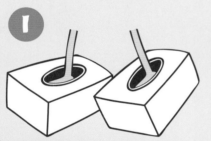

TO MAKE SURE YOUR SHOES FIT, STICK YOUR FEET IN YOUR BOXES. IF YOU'RE USING A TISSUE BOX, HAVE AN ADULT HELPER CUT THE HOLE TO WIDEN IT ENOUGH FOR YOUR FOOT. IF USING A SHOEBOX, CUT AN OVAL-SHAPED HOLE IN THE LID AND TAPE IT DOWN. THEN TAKE YOUR SOON-TO-BE-SHOES OFF FOR THE NEXT PART!

2

CUT YOUR COLORFUL CONSTRUCTION OR TISSUE PAPER INTO SCALES AND GLUE THEM TO COVER THE TOP AND SIDES. TRY NOT TO GLUE ANYTHING ON THE UNDERSIDE OF YOUR SHOE, AS THIS MIGHT MAKE YOUR SHOES TOO SLIPPERY TO USE!

3 CUT SIX TRIANGLES OUT OF ANOTHER SHEET OF WHITE CONSTRUCTION PAPER TO FORM CLAWS.

4

TAPE OR GLUE YOUR CLAWS ONTO ONE END OF YOUR SHOE.

5

NOW SLIP YOUR FEET INSIDE AND **STOMP AWAY!**

IMPORTANT!

EVEN IF YOU AVOID GLUING ANYTHING TO THE BOTTOMS OF YOUR SHOES, THEY MAY BE A LITTLE SLIPPERY ON SMOOTH FLOORS. BE CAREFUL WHEN YOU STOMP AROUND, AND DON'T USE THESE SHOES ON STAIRS!

Many dinos possessed long claws that they used to tear into their prey, or their favorite plants if they were herbivores. Some of the claws were even retractable. Cool! How long did some of these claws get? Up to 2 feet (0.61 m)!

GIVE THE DINOS BELOW SHARP CLAWS, THEN COLOR THEM IN!

25

ORIGAMI ANKYLOSAURUS

1. Take a piece of rectangle–shaped paper (printer paper will do) and fold it in half lengthwise, then unfold.

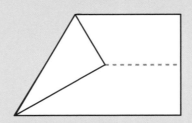

2. Fold the top left corner in towards the crease far enough so that the bottom left corner forms a point.

3. Fold the top right corner over to the left until it meets the left edge of the paper. You should end up with a triangle with a little tail.

4. Fold the bottom right corner under the layer you made in step 3. You should have a perfect triangle now!

 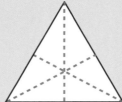

5. Fold the triangle in half and then unfold. Then, rotate the triangle and repeat the fold and unfold. Rotate the triangle once more and repeat the fold and unfold. You should end up with a triangle with several creases.

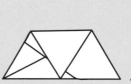 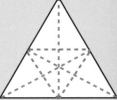

6. Take the top corner and fold it all the way down, until it touches the middle of the bottom edge (use the folds you made in step 5 to help you figure out where the middle is!) and unfold. Fold the right corner over to the left until it touches the middle of the left edge and then unfold. Finally, take the left corner and fold it over to the right until it touches the middle of the right edge. Unfold, then flip your triangle over.

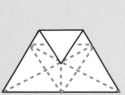 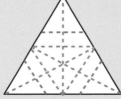

7. Fold the top point so it touches the middle of the triangle, then unfold. Do the same to the other two corners.

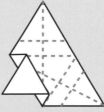 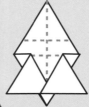

8. Using the creases you made in steps 6 and 7 as a guide, fold the left point over to the right until it touches the middle of the right edge. Then fold the corner back over to the left along the crease you made in step 7. Repeat these folds with the right corner point.

9. Fold the top point down to the bottom point. Then fold the bottom point back up above the crease line you made in step 7, so that the top point is longer than the other five points.

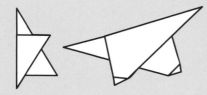

10. Fold your star in half so that all of the folds you did in step 6 are on the inside. Then rotate the figure and stand your dinosaur on its legs. Fold the ends of all four legs up to form the feet.

11. Fold the left point all the way back until it touches your dino's body. (You may need to open your star again to do this.) Then fold the tip forward to form the head.

SAY HELLO TO YOUR DINO!

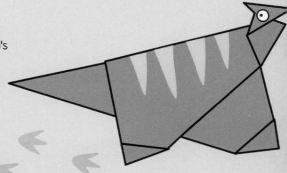

DINO DESIGN SCHOOL

Design your own dinosaur below!
How many legs will it have? What kinds of teeth?
Draw your creation below!

DINOSAUR NAMES SOUND REALLY COMPLICATED BECAUSE THEY'RE SCIENTIFIC, WHICH MEANS THEY DESCRIBE A DINO IN A DIFFERENT LANGUAGE SO SCIENTISTS ACROSS THE WORLD WILL KNOW WHAT IT IS. FOR EXAMPLE, "VELOCIRAPTOR" COMES FROM THE LATIN WORDS FOR "SPEEDY" AND "ROBBER" BECAUSE THE VELOCIRAPTOR WAS PROBABLY EXTREMELY QUICK WHEN IT HUNTED.

WHAT WILL YOU CALL THE DINO YOU'VE JUST CREATED?

MY DINOSAUR'S NAME IS _____

IT MEANS _____

DINOSAUR DEFENSES

Some dinosaurs came equipped with claws, horns, or spikes to drive away predators or catch prey, and other dinosaurs had plates or armor-like hides to shield themselves from attacks. Below is the mighty Giganotosaurus, one of the largest land carnivores ever, on the prowl for a dino-sized meal.

Draw a dino tough enough to beat Giganotosaurus
below, then color in your epic fight scene!

WILL YOUR DINO HAVE CLAWS? SPIKES? TOUGH PLATES? YOU DECIDE!

AS BIG AS A BRONTOSAURUS!

Dinosaurs were pretty big! How big? Check out some comparisons below! Then color each pairing in.

ONE OF THE LARGEST KNOWN CARNIVORES

GIGANOTOSAURUS

(39 to 43 ft/ 12 to 13 m long)

ABOUT AS LONG AS A BUS!

DID YOU KNOW? When it comes to brains, size matters! Stegosaurus might have been 30 feet (9 m) long, but its brain was the size of a walnut. That's a pretty small brain-to-body size ratio, which is why scientists believe it wasn't so smart. On the other hand, raptors and raptor-like dinosaurs, such as Troodon and Bambiraptor, had much larger brains compared to their body sizes, so they were likely fairly intelligent.

SUPERSAURUS

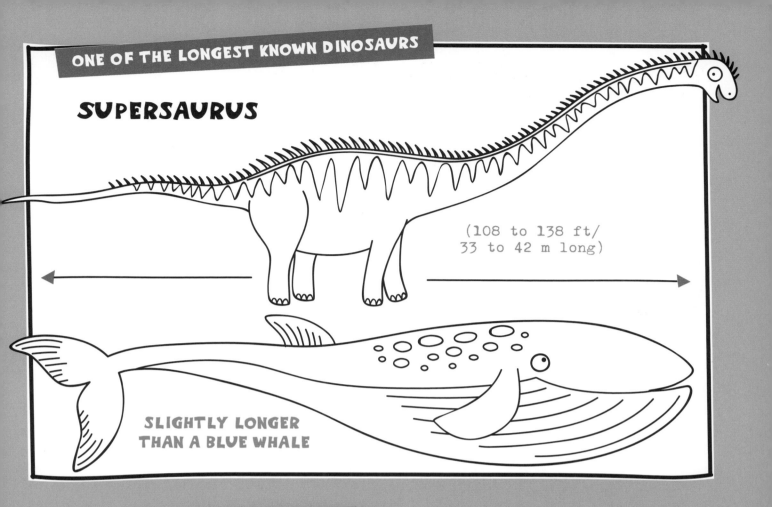

(108 to 138 ft/ 33 to 42 m long)

SLIGHTLY LONGER THAN A BLUE WHALE

SAUROPOSEIDON

(59 ft/18 m tall, with its neck extended)

AS TALL AS A SIX STORY BUILDING

HOW MUCH DOES A DINOSAUR WEIGH?

Argentinosaurus was probably the heaviest known dinosaur. It weighed about 90 tons, or about as much as 18 elephants! On the scales below, draw lots of heavy things to balance out the dino on the next page. Then, color them all in!

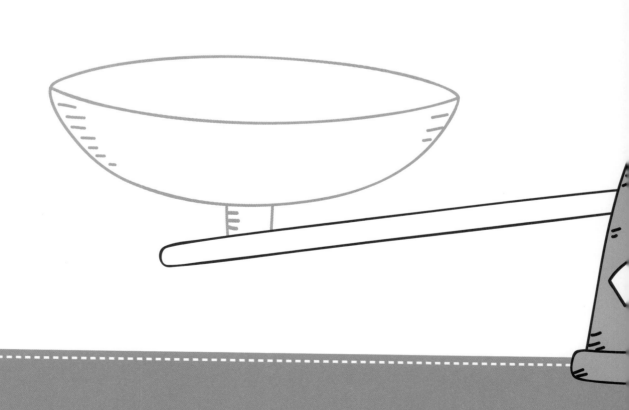

DID YOU KNOW? Our modern-day birds are descended from dinosaurs, so the shortest, lightest, and smallest dinos are the currently-living hummingbirds. The smallest known non-bird dinosaur was Parvicursor remotus, a tiny Cretaceous dino that measured 15 inches (39 cm) long and 5.7 ounces (162 g) in weight—smaller than a chicken!

Argentinosaurus

YOUR TRIP THROUGH TIME CONTINUES!
DRAW YOURSELF RIDING YOUR FAVORITE DINO FRIEND, THEN FILL
THE REST OF THIS SCENE WITH MORE PREHISTORIC PALS.
WHEN YOU'RE DONE, DON'T FORGET TO COLOR IT ALL IN!

35

SUDOKUSAURUS

Thinking about becoming a paleontologist? Then you'll probably want to sharpen your observational and puzzle-solving skills! Complete the boxes below by drawing in the missing symbols.
Each symbol can only appear once in each row, column, or diagonal.

MEGALOSAUR FILL-IN-THE-BLANKS

On the following pages, you'll find a story that's missing more than a few words! The blanks below match those missing words on the next page. Fill them in without peeking, then turn the page and copy your words into the story, in the order they're listed below.

1. _____ (your name)
2. _____ (noun)
3. _____ (your name)
4. _____ (nature word)
5. _____ (adjective)
6. _____ (number)
7. _____ (number)
8. _____ (body parts)
9. _____ (verb)
10. _____ (adjective)
11. _____ (food)
12. _____ (body parts)
13. _____ (verb)
14. _____ (verb)
15. _____ (noun)
16. _____ (year)
17. _____ (nature words)
18. _____ (name of a job)
19. _____ (noun)
20. _____ (your name)
21. _____ (action)
22. _____ (noun)
23. _____ (your name)
24. _____ (noun)
25. _____ (dinosaur name)
26. _____ (name of an adult you know)
27. _____ (adjective)

THE MIGHTY -SAURUS

----
1. your name

LONG, LONG AGO, DURING THE _____ PERIOD, THE MIGHTY _____-SAURUS
                                2. noun   3. your name

ROAMED THE _____. IT WAS A _____ BEAST,
                4. nature word   5. adjective

STANDING AT _____ FEET HIGH AND WEIGHING _____ POUNDS
                6. number   7. number

IT HAD MASSIVE _____, WHICH IT USED TO _____.
                8. body parts   9. verb

THIS DINOSAUR PREFERRED _____ CLIMATES, WHERE IT HUNTED ITS FAVORITE MEAL,
                            10. adjective

_____, WITH ITS SHARP _____.
    11. food   12. body parts

WHEN IT WASN'T HUNTING, IT LIKED TO _____ OR _____.
                                        13. verb   14. verb

SCIENTISTS FIRST DISCOVERED ITS EXISTENCE WHEN THEY UNCOVERED ITS FOSSILIZED _____
                                                                                15. noun

IN _____. THESE FOSSILS WERE FOUND IN WHAT HAD ONCE BEEN _____,
    16. year   17. nature words

BY A _____ WHO HAD BEEN LOOKING FOR A _____.
        18. name of a job   19. noun

ROAR!!

38

SCIENTISTS BELIEVE THAT THIS PARTICULAR _____-SAURUS WAS TRYING TO
20. your name

_____ AT THE TIME IT WAS BURIED IN _____.
21. action   22. noun

WHILE SCIENTISTS AREN'T ENTIRELY SURE HOW THE DINOSAURS WERE WIPED OFF THE FACE OF THE PLANET,

THERE ARE SEVERAL THEORIES ABOUT HOW THE _____-SAURUS DISAPPEARED.
23. your name

THE MOST POPULAR OF THESE THEORIES IS THAT THEY WERE ALL KILLED BY A FALLING

_____, ALTHOUGH OTHERS SAY THAT THEY WERE HUNTED TO EXTINCTION BY
24. noun

EITHER THE _____ OR THE _____-SAURUS.
25. dinosaur name   26. name of an adult you know

WHAT A _____ DINOSAUR!
27. adjective

FOSSiL FiELDS

On these pages, you'll find
an entire field of fossils.
How many of each can you dig up?
Once you've found all of them, color them in!

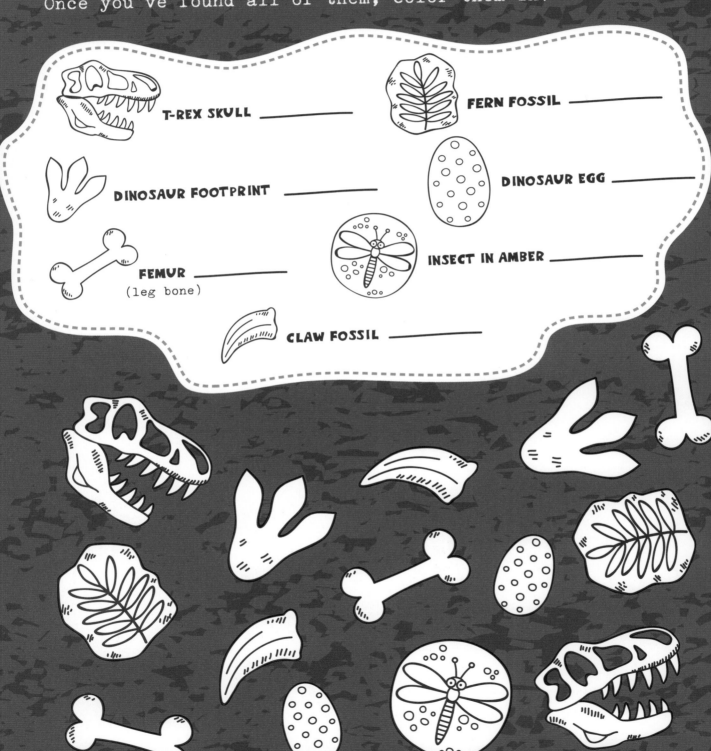

T-REX SKULL _____

FERN FOSSIL _____

DINOSAUR FOOTPRINT _____

DINOSAUR EGG _____

FEMUR _____
(leg bone)

INSECT IN AMBER _____

CLAW FOSSIL _____

There are many ways fossils can form, but one of the most common is when a dinosaur (or any other creature) dies and ends up buried in mud or silt. Almost everything rots away quickly, but the bones, being hard, are instead buried by more and more sediment. As they're buried, minerals seep in and replace each cell. What's left are petrified bones!

DiG iT

STEP I: FINDING THE FOSSIL

Add more bones and rocks to this underground scene!

Fossils can be found a variety of ways. Sometimes, scientists look in places where the geology is suitable or where fossils have already been found. Other times, people stumble across fossils accidentally.

STEP 2: EXCAVATING THE FOSSIL

Before a fossil can be shipped off to a museum, a paleontologist (scientist who studies fossils) decides whether or not it should be dug up. (By the way, this is why the place where a fossil is excavated is called a dig!) If it should, the rock around it is removed carefully using picks, rock hammers, and even brushes to dust away dirt.

Find the fossils in the field of rocks below, add some of your own, and color them all in.

STEP 3: TRANSPORTING THE FOSSIL

After notes are taken on where the fossil was located (including the rock layer that had housed it), the fossil is transported to a museum. Help the fossil go from the dig site to the museum by working your way through this maze!

STEP 4: STUDYING THE FOSSIL

Once at the museum and cleaned, each fossil is catalogued by scientists who look them over, study them under microscopes, and compare them to bones of living and extinct animals.

Complete the skeleton below by drawing in the missing bones!

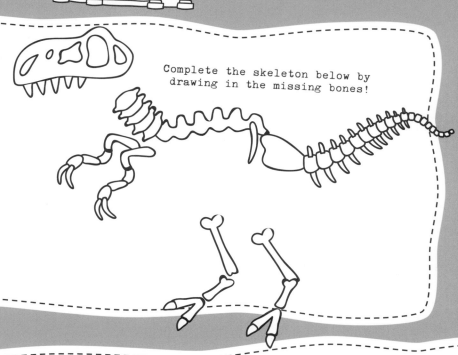

STEP 5: DISPLAYING THE FOSSIL

Did you know? Only a few fossils or casts (copies of fossils) are ever displayed in a museum. These are usually ones that have been heavily studied, carefully reassembled, and mounted for the public so everyone can check them out.

Color the dinosaur display below!

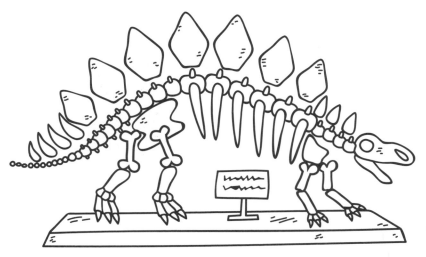

43

MAKE YOUR OWN FOSSIL

YOU WILL NEED:

2 CUPS FLOUR

1 CUP WATER

1 CUP USED COFFEE GROUNDS

1 CUP SALT

PLASTIC DINOSAURS OR OTHER PLASTIC OBJECTS YOU WANT TO "FOSSILIZE"

TIP: IF YOU'D LIKE DARKER ROCKS, CONSIDER ADDING JUST A LITTLE BIT OF COLD COFFEE AS WELL!

1 Mix the flour, water, coffee, and salt in a bowl until you've made a soft dough.

2 When your dough is soft and putty-like enough to use, take a handful and press one plastic "fossil" into the dough. Add more dough on top until you can completely cover the dinosaur, then roll the dough ball into a smooth rock shape.

3 Wet your fingers with water and run them over the surface to make sure your rock is smooth.

4 Place your rocks on a baking sheet (covered with parchment paper) and let them dry for a day. If you can't wait to excavate, ask an adult helper to bake your rocks for 3 hours in an oven heated to 200° F/93° C. Have them turn the rocks every half hour to make sure they're baked on all sides.

5 When hardened, use a butter knife "chisel" to excavate your dinosaur and a paintbrush to brush off the dust—just like a real paleontologist!

Sketch your fossil findings
(like a real paleontologist) below!

HOW DO SCIENTISTS KNOW WHAT DINOSAURS LOOKED LIKE?

They guess, based on skeletons and other traces dinosaurs left behind!

Below are dinosaur bones. What do you think these dinos looked like when they were alive? Draw your own dinosaurs over these bones, using each skeleton as a guide!

(NO) BONES ABOUT IT!

Below are a bunch of bones, ready for identification. Which dinos do they belong to? Untangle the lines to find out!

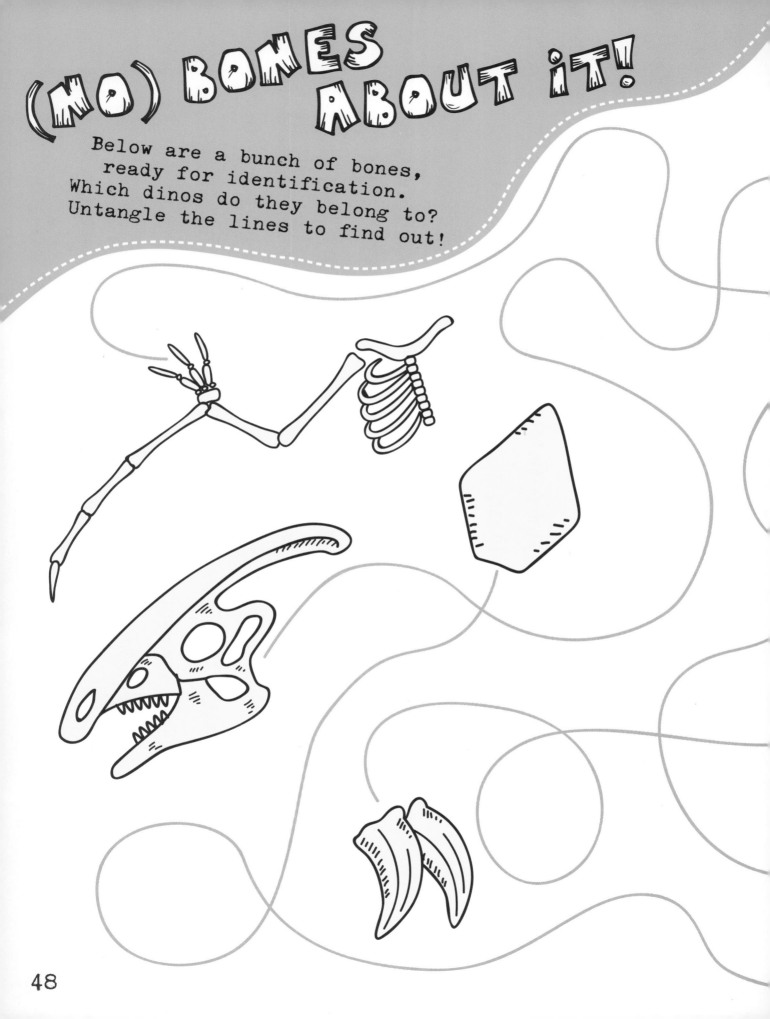

LIVING FINDS!

Aardvark
Coelacanth
Crocodile
Dragonfly
Frilled Shark
Hagfish
Horseshoe Crab
Lungfish
Mantis Shrimp
Mosquito
Nautilus
Okapi
Platypus
Purple Frog
Salamander
Scallop
Skate
Solenodon
Spider
Starfish
Tuatara
Turtle
Urchin
Vampire Squid

The living fossils on the previous page are hidden in the word search below. Find them by looking forward, backward, up, down, and diagonally. Then when you're done, color these pages in.

```
A S B V K F T M G U Y L S K A T E F Z M F
M T O Q N I R Y A D A R A T A U T K B R Q
R D J M F R H F U F E P L J V Q J K H M K
E P Y Y S V O T Y N F Y U U B G U Q T A Y
D U X F O A R S Y B F L D R N P B H Y J O
I J M V L M S P H M K K V C P G H C C T M
P D K Q E P E S U L I T U A N L F Y U I U
S T E A N I S G D Z F L R S S V E I Q G E
M V A Y O R H F G P B K W V H D E F S S A
A I A H D E O U A Z L G S A T F X C R H A
N K R C O S E R K R J A G I R I N O L O R
T A D R N Q C C S V D F T I O O S E F M G
I D V O U U R H A A I T L Y T U E L K P N
S R A C X I A I Y S L L U I P V I A N X M
S A R O H D B N H T E A U R E U V C S X I
H G K D X G J W K D L Q M W T V S A C B Z
R O Z I O S T O S I S O L A G L Z N A P M
I N I L Q Y Y H K O O R E E N Y E T L G T
M F F E W Y A C M A L T V N Y D C H L D U
P L S U N R E E W D P S L H K S E W O N X
J Y C K K W S T A R F I S H X H J R P D Z
```

D YOU KNOW? Evolution is a process in which, over thousands or millions of ars, a species completely changes. Now and then, animals are born with certain aits that help them survive better than members of the same species. Members th the trait survive to have babies more often than those without the trait. is specific process is called natural selection.

51

EGG-XACT MATCHES!

Each of the eggs below has a perfect twin, save for one. Find and circle the lone egg, then color the others in matching colors!

52

BIRDS, THE MODERN DINOSAURS

To solve the word puzzles below, change only a single letter in each step until you get from one thing to another. The clues will make this easier for you. Good luck!

1. HELP THE DINO EVOLVE INTO A BIRD!

DINO

_ _ _ _   CLUE: ANOTHER WORD FOR "EAT"
_ _ _ _   CLUE: THIS CAN MEAN "OKAY" OR "FANCY."
_ _ _ _   CLUE: WHEN YOU LOCATE SOMETHING, YOU _ _ _ _ _ IT.
_ _ _ _   CLUE: A FANCY WORD FOR TYING SOMETHING TOGETHER

BIRD

2. WHAT DO WORMS EAT?

WORM

_ _ _ _   CLUE: OPPOSITE OF COOL
_ _ _ _   CLUE: A BUMP ON YOUR SKIN. SOME PEOPLE THINK TOADS GIVE YOU THIS.
_ _ _ _   CLUE: A POINTED THING YOU THROW AT A TARGET
_ _ _ _   CLUE: THE THING THAT WORMS EAT (AND LIVE IN!)

3. WHAT SCARED THE RAT?

RAT

_ _ _   CLUE: IF YOU LEAVE FRUIT OUT FOR TOO LONG, IT'LL DO THIS.
_ _ _   CLUE: MANY OF SOMETHING IS A _ _ _ _ _ _.
_ _ _   CLUE: SHORT FOR "LAUGH OUT LOUD"
_ _ _   CLUE: SHORT FOR "LITTLE"
_ _ _   CLUE: CARS NEED THIS TO RUN.
_ _ _   CLUE: NIGHT BIRDS. THEY EAT RATS!

4. HELP THE TREE PRODUCE A SEED!

TREE

_ _ _ _   CLUE: AN OLD WAY OF SAYING "YOU"
_ _ _ _   CLUE: A TIME-BASED WORD: _ _ _ _ _ AND NOW
_ _ _ _   CLUE: ANYONE WHO'S 13 YEARS OLD TO 19 YEARS OLD
_ _ _ _   CLUE: IF YOU SAW SOMETHING, YOU HAVE _ _ _ _ _ _ IT.

SEED

LET'S GO MODERN-DAY DINO HUNTING!

LOOK OUT YOUR WINDOW AND USE THIS PAGE TO SKETCH ANY MODERN-DAY DINOS YOU SEE (AKA BIRDS). IF YOU CAN'T SEE ANY MODERN-DAY DINOS FROM WHERE YOU ARE, USE THIS PAGE TO DRAW A BIRD, THEN GIVE IT THE FACE AND CLAWS OF A DINOSAUR. THEN COLOR THEM IN!

FIND THE FOSSILS

ON THE PAGES BELOW, THERE ARE:

10 horseshoe crabs
9 nautiluses
8 eggs
7 scallops
6 spiders
5 femur bones

CAN YOU FIND THEM ALL?
COLOR THE SCENE!

FILL THIS SCENE WITH PREHISTORIC PALS, THEN COLOR IT IN!

DID YOU KNOW?

Scientists aren't completely sure what wiped the dinosaurs out, but a lot of evidence suggests that a giant meteorite crashed down in what is now Mexico. This meteorite kicked up so much dust and triggered so much volcanic activity that the climate changed. Three-quarters of all life on Earth, from plants to giant sea-dwelling reptiles, died out. Of all the dinosaurs, only a few bird species could adapt and survive.

CRAFTY CROSSWORDS

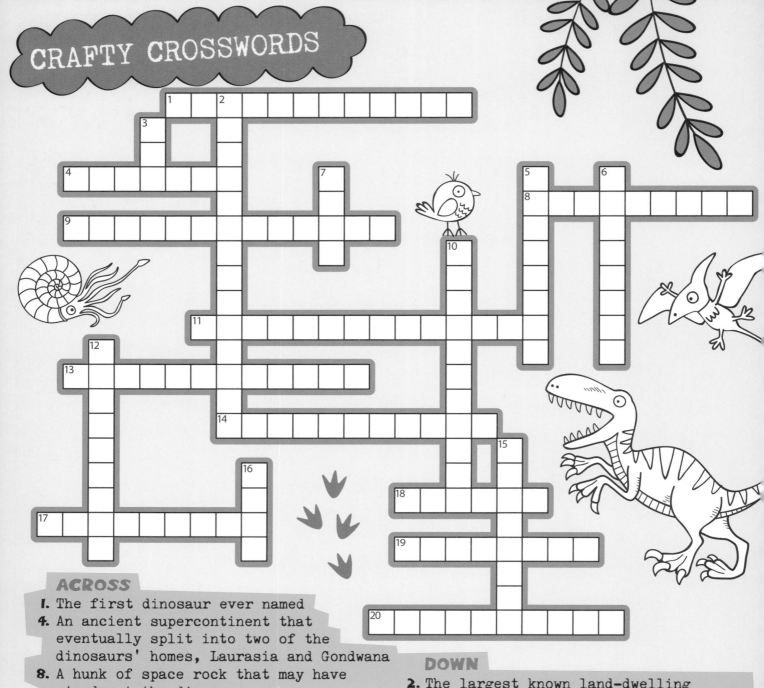

ACROSS

1. The first dinosaur ever named
4. An ancient supercontinent that eventually split into two of the dinosaurs' homes, Laurasia and Gondwana
8. A hunk of space rock that may have wiped out the dinosaurs
9. Feathered creature with the features of both dinosaurs and birds
11. A person who studies ancient creatures
13. A small but quick dinosaur whose name means "speedy robber"
14. Probably the longest known dinosaur
17. A creature that mostly eats meat
18. The petrified remains or impression of a prehistoric creature
19. Period in which many new species of plants and animals first appeared
20. The last period of the reign of the dinosaurs

DOWN

2. The largest known land-dwelling meat-eater that ever lived
3. Place where fossils are excavated
5. An ancient squid relative that once lived in a North American sea
6. The era during which the dinosaurs lived
7. A modern-day dinosaur
10. A dinosaur known for two things: its distinctive plates and its walnut-sized brain
12. A creature that mostly eats plants
15. A dry, desert-filled time period that kicked off the reign of the dinosaurs
16. Nickname for the mighty Tyrannosaurus rex

ROAR!!

DECORATE
THIS
DINO FRIEND
AND COLOR
HIM IN!

ANSWERS

THE WILD WORLD OF DINOSAURS
Pages 6-7

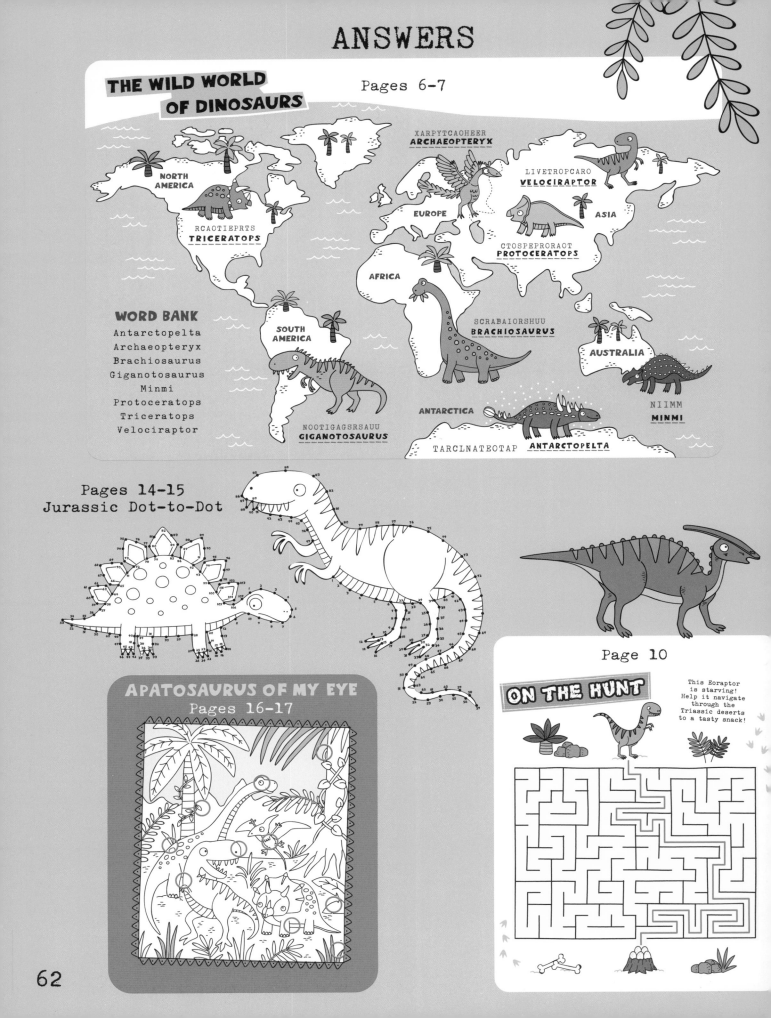

NORTH AMERICA

RCAOTIEPRTS
TRICERATOPS

XARPYTCAOHEER
ARCHAEOPTERYX

LIVETROPCARO
VELOCIRAPTOR

EUROPE

ASIA

CTOSPEPRORAOT
PROTOCERATOPS

AFRICA

SCRABAIORSHUU
BRACHIOSAURUS

AUSTRALIA

WORD BANK
Antarctopelta
Archaeopteryx
Brachiosaurus
Giganotosaurus
Minmi
Protoceratops
Triceratops
Velociraptor

SOUTH AMERICA

NOOTIGAGSRSAUU
GIGANOTOSAURUS

ANTARCTICA

NIIMM
MINMI

TARCLNATEOTAP **ANTARCTOPELTA**

Pages 14-15
Jurassic Dot-to-Dot

APATOSAURUS OF MY EYE
Pages 16-17

Page 10

ON THE HUNT

This Eoraptor is starving! Help it navigate through the Triassic deserts to a tasty snack!

Page 36 Sudokusaurus

Pages 40-41

FOSSIL FIELDS

On these pages, you'll find an entire field of fossils. How many of each can you dig up? Once you've found all of them, color them in!

T-REX SKULL	6	FERN FOSSIL — 5
DINOSAUR FOOT PRINT	5	DINOSAUR EGG — 6
FEMUR	6	INSECT IN AMBER — 5
CLAW FOSSIL	6	

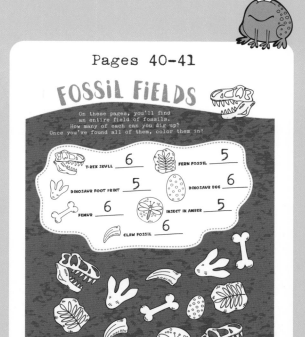

Pages 48-49

(NO) BONES ABOUT IT!

Below are a bunch of bones, ready for identification. Which dinos do they belong to? Untangle the lines to find out!

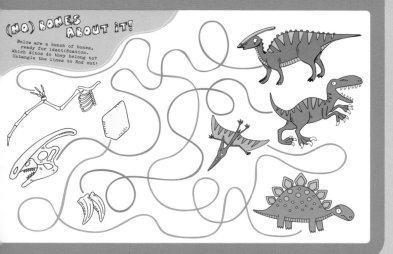

Pages 42-43
Dig It

STEP 3:
TRANSPORTING THE FOSSIL

STEP 4:
STUDYING THE FOSSIL

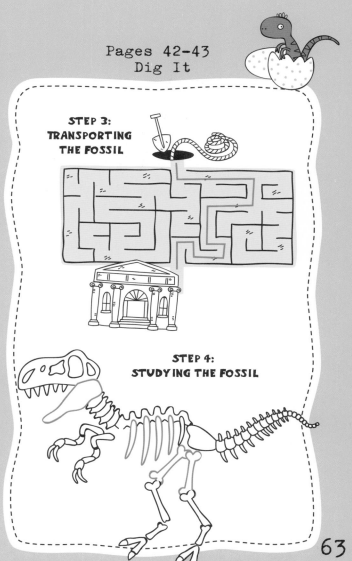

Page 51
Living Finds

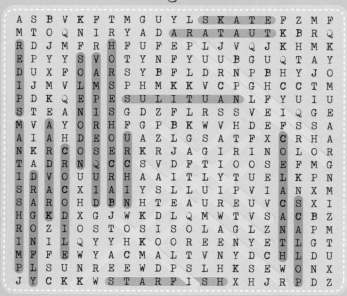

```
A S B V K F T M G U Y L S K A T E F Z M F
M T O Q N I R Y A D A R A T A U T K B R Q
R D J M F R H F U F E P L J V Q J K H M K
E P Y Y S V O T Y N F Y U U B G U Q T A Y
D U X F O A R S Y B F L D R N P B H Y J M
I J M K L M S P H M K K V C P G H C C T M
P D K Q E P E S U L I T U A N L F Y U I U
S T E A N I S G D Z F L R S S V E I Q G E
M A V A Y R E H F G P B K W V H D E F S A
A N I A R O H O U A Z L G S A T F X C R H
T K A R N Q R K R J A G I R I N O L O L M
I D V R O U U R C S V D F T I O O S E F M
S R A O H U I A A I T L Y T U E L M C X I
H A G K D B N H T E A U R E U V C S X X M
R G O I X G J W K D L Q M W T V S A C Z B
I O Z I O S T O S I S O L A G L Z N Q Z I
M N I L Q Y Y H K O O R E E N E Y E T L D
P F E W Y A C M A L T V N Y D C H L D T U
L Y S U N R E E W D P S L H K S E W O N X
J Y C K K W S T A R F I S H X H J R P D Z
```

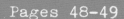

63

BIRDS, THE MODERN DINOSAURS

1. HELP THE DINO EVOLVE INTO A BIRD!

DINO
DINE CLUE: ANOTHER WORD FOR "EAT"
FINE CLUE: THIS CAN MEAN "OKAY" OR "FANCY."
FIND CLUE: WHEN YOU LOCATE SOMETHING, YOU **FIND** IT.
BIND CLUE: A FANCY WORD FOR TYING SOMETHING TOGETHER
BIRD

2. WHAT DO WORMS EAT?

WORM
WARM CLUE: OPPOSITE OF COOL
WART CLUE: BUMPS ON YOUR SKIN. SOME PEOPLE THINK TOADS GIVE YOU THIS.
DART CLUE: A POINTED THING YOU THROW AT A TARGET
DIRT CLUE: THE THING THAT WORMS EAT (AND LIVE IN!)

3. WHAT SCARED THE RAT?

RAT
ROT CLUE: IF YOU LEAVE FRUIT OUT FOR TOO LONG, IT'LL DO THIS.
LOT CLUE: MANY OF SOMETHING IS A **LOT**.
LOL CLUE: SHORT FOR "LAUGH OUT LOUD"
LIL CLUE: SHORT FOR "LITTLE"
OIL CLUE: CARS NEED THIS TO RUN.
OWL CLUE: NIGHT BIRDS. THEY EAT RATS!

4. HELP THE TREE PRODUCE A SEED!

TREE
THEE CLUE: AN OLD WAY OF SAYING "YOU"
THEN CLUE: A TIME-BASED WORD: **THEN** AND NOW
TEEN CLUE: ANYONE WHO'S 13 YEARS OLD TO 19 YEARS OLD
SEEN CLUE: IF YOU SAW SOMETHING, YOU HAVE **SEEN** IT.
SEED

EGG-XACT MATCHES!

CRAFTY CROSSWORDS — Page 60

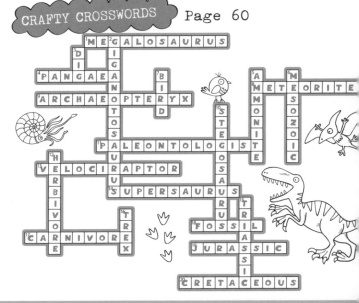

FIND THE FOSSILS

 HORSESHOE CRABS

 NAUTILUSES

 EGGS

 SCALLOPS

 SPIDERS

 FEMUR BONES